Caravan Jo

Introducti(

In memory of Otis, Lucie and Benni, our beloved dogs who so enjoyed being out in our caravan on our travels around the United Kingdom, running free through woodlands, fields and chasing squirrels (they never caught any), exploring the picturesque countryside and having a great fun time out in the fresh air. They truly loved being away in our caravan and the joy to their lives that that lifestyle brought.

On our travels over the years, we, like many other caravanners have always kept a travel record, or journal of our adventures. Ours having being recorded in a plain notebook. However, over the years we have found that a plain white sheet of paper is quite uninspiring, so I set about searching the shops and the internet trying to find something a little more interesting, but drew a blank.

SO, I decided to create my own. I wanted a journal that would be colourful, fun and inviting with a light-hearted feel to it to show the social, fun, quirky side of caravanning. Together with Kate, from Kate Smith Designs, we have interpreted my original concept into this beautiful caravanning journal you are now holding and we have brought my idea to life.

In this caravanning journal, you will see there are plenty of pages in which to record your travels and adventures, interspersed with colourful, light hearted and amusing images of caravan life and all it encompasses, throughout the book. At the back of the journal is a large map of the British Isles, so you can pinpoint the areas visited on your adventures.

I hope you will find this journal useful, fun and inspirational. Then on the cold and wet days of Winter, you can look back through your memories and relive the happy times of your adventures, for years to come. Happy travels!

Kind regards,
Carol xx
Leisure Logs Caravan Journal

'With thanks to Jean Hills for her help and advice for giving my text the once over'

Date:

Destination:

Sea

Caravan
Park

Date:

Destination:

Sea

Caravan Park

Date:

Destination:

Sea

Caravan Park

Date:

Destination:

Sea

Caravan Park

Date:

Destination:

Date:

Destination:

Date:

Destination:

Date:

Destination:

Sea

Caravan Park

Date:

Destination:

Sea

Caravan Park

Date:

Destination:

Date:

Destination:

Date:

Destination:

Sea

Caravan
Park

Date:

Destination:

Date:

Destination:

Sea

Caravan Park

Date:

Destination:

Date:

Destination:

Date:

Destination:

Sea

Caravan Park

Date:

Destination:

Sea

Caravan Park

Date:

Destination:

Sea

Caravan Park

Date:

Destination:

Date:

Destination:

Date:

Destination:

Sea

Caravan
Park

Date:

Destination:

Date:
Destination:

Sea

Caravan Park

Date:

Destination:

Sea

Caravan Park

Date:

Destination:

Sea   Caravan Park

Date:

Destination:

Sea

Caravan Park

Date:

Destination:

Sea

Caravan Park

Date:

Destination:

Sea

Caravan Park

Date:

Destination:

Date:

Destination:

Sea   Caravan Park

Date:

Destination:

Sea

Caravan Park

Date:

Destination:

Sea

Caravan Park

Date:

Destination:

Sea

Caravan Park

Date:

Destination:

EARLY MORNING SPRINKLE & PAT

Date:

Destination:

Date:

Destination:

Sea

Caravan
Park

Date:

Destination:

Date:

Destination:

Sea

Caravan
Park

Date:

Destination:

Date:

Destination:

Date:

Destination:

Sea

Caravan
Park

Date:

Destination:

Date:

Destination:

Sea

Caravan Park

Date:

Destination:

Date:

Destination:

Sea

Caravan Park

Date:

Destination:

Sea

Caravan Park

Date:

Destination:

Date:

Destination:

Sea

Caravan Park

Date:

Destination:

Date:

Destination:

Sea | Caravan Park

Date:

Destination:

Sea

Caravan Park

Date:

Destination:

Date:

Destination:

Sea

Caravan
Park

Date:

Destination:

Shetlands

Orkneys

Hebrides

SCOTLAND

BRITISH ISLES